Mushroom Millions: Fungi For

Table Of Contents

Chapter 1: Introduction to Mushroom Cultivation — 9

The Rise of Urban Mushroom Farming — 9

Benefits of Growing Mushrooms at Home — 13

Chapter 2: Getting Started with Home Mushroom Cultivation — 16

Essential Equipment and Supplies — 16

www.farmers-library.com

Mushroom Millions: Fungi Fortunes from Small Spaces

Choosing the Right Mushroom Varieties — 19

Setting Up Your Growing Space — 23

Chapter 3: Specialty Mushroom Varieties for Urban Farmers — 26

Gourmet Mushrooms: A Culinary Delight — 26

Medicinal Mushrooms: Health Benefits and Uses — 29

Exotic Varieties: Expanding Your Offerings — 32

Mushroom Millions: Fungi Fortunes from Small Spaces

Chapter 4: DIY Mushroom Growing Kits for Small Spaces — 35

- Designing Your Own Kits — 35
- Sourcing Materials and Supplies — 38
- Step-by-Step Kit Assembly — 41

Chapter 5: Organic Mushroom Farming Techniques — 44

- Soil and Substrate Preparation — 44
- Pest and Disease Management — 47

Mushroom Millions: Fungi Fortunes from Small Spaces

Sustainable Practices in Organic Farming — 50

Chapter 6: Vertical Farming Solutions for Mushroom Production — 53

Understanding Vertical Farming Concepts — 53

Designing Vertical Systems for Mushrooms — 56

Benefits of Vertical Farming in Urban Settings — 59

Chapter 7: Gourmet Mushrooms for Restaurants and Chefs — 62

Identifying Market Opportunities	62
Building Relationships with Local Restaurants	65
Pricing and Packaging Strategies	68

Chapter 8: Medicinal Mushrooms and Their Commercial Potential — 71

Overview of Medicinal Mushroom Varieties	71
Market Trends and Consumer Demand	74

Regulations and Safety Considerations — 77

Chapter 9: Sustainable Practices in Mushroom Farming — 79

Environmental Benefits of Mushroom Cultivation — 79

Waste Reduction and Recycling Techniques — 83

Community Engagement and Education — 86

Chapter 10: Online Marketing Strategies for Mushroom Entrepreneurs — 90

Mushroom Millions: Fungi Fortunes from Small Spaces

Building Your Brand Online	90
Social Media and Content Marketing	93
E-commerce Platforms for Selling Mushrooms	96
Chapter 11: Scaling Your Mushroom Business	**99**
Expanding Production Capacity	99
Diversifying Product Lines	102
Collaborations and Partnerships	105

Chapter 12: Future Trends in Mushroom Farming — 108

Innovations in Cultivation Techniques — 108

Market Predictions and Opportunities — 111

The Role of Technology in Mushroom Production — 114

Chapter 13: Conclusion and Next Steps — 117

Recap of Key Takeaways — 117

Resources for Continued Learning — 120

Encouragement for the Journey Ahead — 123

Mushroom Millions: Fungi Fortunes from Small Spaces

Chapter 1: Introduction to Mushroom Cultivation

The Rise of Urban Mushroom Farming

The rise of urban mushroom farming represents a transformative shift in agricultural practices, especially within metropolitan areas where space is often limited. As cities continue to grow, there is an increasing demand for locally sourced food, and mushrooms present an ideal solution. They require significantly less space than traditional crops, can thrive on organic waste products, and provide a rapid return on investment. Urban dwellers are discovering that they can cultivate mushrooms in basements, garages, and even on rooftops, making them an appealing option for small-scale farmers and entrepreneurs looking to capitalize on the growing interest in sustainable food sources.

In addition to their practicality, mushrooms are versatile and can be cultivated in various forms, including gourmet, medicinal, and specialty varieties. This diversity allows urban farmers to cater to a wide range of markets.

Mushroom Millions: Fungi Fortunes from Small Spaces

Gourmet mushrooms like shiitake, oyster, and lion's mane are increasingly sought after by restaurants and health-conscious consumers. Meanwhile, the medicinal properties of certain mushrooms, such as reishi and chaga, are gaining popularity among wellness enthusiasts. This trend not only opens up new avenues for profit but also encourages urban farmers to educate themselves on the benefits and uses of different mushroom types, enhancing their marketability.

The emergence of DIY mushroom growing kits has further fueled the interest in urban mushroom farming. These kits, which are designed for ease of use, allow individuals with minimal experience to cultivate their own mushrooms at home. This accessibility is particularly appealing to side hustle entrepreneurs and sustainable living enthusiasts who seek to grow their own food while minimizing their environmental impact. As these kits become more popular, they also foster a sense of community among urban growers, encouraging knowledge sharing and collaboration.

Mushroom Millions: Fungi Fortunes from Small Spaces

Vertical farming solutions have also played a crucial role in the rise of urban mushroom farming. By utilizing vertical space, growers can maximize their yields and make efficient use of limited urban environments. This method allows for higher production rates in smaller areas, making it feasible for aspiring mushroom farmers to establish profitable operations without requiring large expanses of land. Furthermore, vertical farming can be integrated with sustainable practices, such as composting and recycling agricultural waste, promoting environmentally friendly operations that resonate with modern consumers.

As urban mushroom farming continues to gain traction, online marketing strategies are becoming increasingly important for entrepreneurs in this niche. Social media platforms, e-commerce websites, and local farmers' markets provide avenues for growers to showcase their products and connect with potential customers. By leveraging these tools, small-scale farmers can build their brand and establish a loyal customer base.

Mushroom Millions: Fungi Fortunes from Small Spaces

This digital engagement not only enhances sales but also raises awareness of the benefits of mushrooms, paving the way for a thriving urban farming community focused on sustainability, health, and innovation.

Mushroom Millions: Fungi Fortunes from Small Spaces

Benefits of Growing Mushrooms at Home

Growing mushrooms at home offers a range of benefits that cater to diverse interests and lifestyles, making it an appealing venture for anyone from urban homesteaders to aspiring food entrepreneurs. One of the most significant advantages is the ability to cultivate fresh, gourmet mushrooms right in your kitchen or backyard, ensuring a constant supply of high-quality produce. This not only enhances culinary experiences but also reduces reliance on store-bought mushrooms, which may lack flavor and freshness. By growing specialty varieties such as shiitake, oyster, or lion's mane, enthusiasts can elevate their dishes and attract the attention of local restaurants and chefs seeking unique ingredients.

In addition to culinary benefits, home mushroom cultivation provides an opportunity for sustainable living. Mushrooms can be grown using minimal resources and can thrive in small spaces, making them an ideal crop for urban and suburban environments. Many mushroom varieties can be cultivated using waste materials, such as coffee grounds or straw, promoting a zero-waste lifestyle.

Mushroom Millions: Fungi Fortunes from Small Spaces

This not only contributes to environmental sustainability but also allows growers to engage in eco-friendly practices that resonate with the growing consumer demand for organic and sustainable products.

The economic potential of growing mushrooms at home cannot be overlooked. For side hustle entrepreneurs and small-scale farmers, mushrooms represent a lucrative opportunity. With relatively low startup costs for DIY mushroom growing kits and minimal maintenance requirements, individuals can tap into a profitable market. Specialty mushrooms are gaining popularity among health-conscious consumers and gourmet chefs alike, creating demand that can be met through local sales or online platforms. The ability to sell directly to consumers or establish partnerships with local businesses can significantly enhance profitability.

Moreover, cultivating mushrooms at home can serve as a gateway to learning and experimentation. For wellness entrepreneurs and those interested in medicinal mushrooms, home cultivation provides the chance to explore the health benefits of various species.

Mushroom Millions: Fungi Fortunes from Small Spaces

By growing mushrooms known for their medicinal properties, individuals can educate themselves and others about their uses, from enhancing immune health to providing natural remedies. This knowledge can be translated into new business opportunities, such as workshops, informational blogs, or even product lines centered around health and wellness.

Finally, growing mushrooms at home fosters a sense of community and connection. As sustainable practices and local food movements gain traction, mushroom growers can join networks and share experiences, tips, and best practices. Online forums, social media groups, and local workshops offer platforms for collaboration and support, enhancing the overall experience of mushroom cultivation. This sense of belonging can be particularly appealing for urban and suburban dwellers who seek to cultivate not only food but also relationships within their communities. As more individuals embrace mushroom cultivation, the potential for innovation and shared success within this niche continues to grow, making it an exciting time to embark on this journey.

Chapter 2: Getting Started with Home Mushroom Cultivation

Essential Equipment and Supplies

In the realm of mushroom cultivation, having the right equipment and supplies is fundamental to ensuring a successful growing operation. For aspiring mycologists and small-scale farmers, the initial investment in essential tools can significantly influence the quality and yield of the mushrooms produced. Key items include sterilization equipment, such as pressure cookers or autoclaves, which are crucial for preparing substrates free from contaminants. Additionally, high-quality growing containers, whether they are plastic bags, jars, or specialized mushroom bags, provide an ideal environment for mycelium to flourish. These foundational supplies set the stage for healthy mushroom growth, making them indispensable for both beginners and seasoned growers.

Temperature and humidity control are vital factors in mushroom cultivation, making environmental monitoring equipment essential.

Mushroom Millions: Fungi Fortunes from Small Spaces

Thermometers, hygrometers, and digital controllers help maintain the optimal conditions for various mushroom species. For instance, shiitake mushrooms thrive in cooler temperatures, while oyster mushrooms prefer warmth. Moreover, investing in humidifiers or misting systems can aid in maintaining the necessary moisture levels that promote robust fruiting bodies. An understanding of the specific requirements for different mushroom varieties will enhance production efficiency and ultimately contribute to profitability.

In addition to environmental controls, growers must consider the importance of substrate materials. The choice of substrate directly impacts the nutrient profile available to the mushrooms. Common substrates include sawdust, straw, and coffee grounds, each offering unique benefits depending on the mushroom species being cultivated. Organic options are increasingly popular among consumers, aligning with sustainable practices that enhance marketability. For entrepreneurs looking to carve out a niche, sourcing local or organic substrates not only supports sustainability but can also attract a more discerning customer base.

Mushroom Millions: Fungi Fortunes from Small Spaces

As the market for gourmet and medicinal mushrooms expands, effective packaging and branding tools become essential for successful sales. Invest in eco-friendly packaging that not only preserves freshness but also resonates with the values of sustainability-focused consumers. Labels that clearly communicate the unique benefits of the mushroom varieties, such as nutritional information or medicinal properties, can attract interest from restaurants and health-conscious buyers. Additionally, utilizing photography and digital marketing tools allows mushroom entrepreneurs to showcase the beauty of their products, engaging potential customers through social media platforms and online marketplaces.

Finally, educational materials and resources play a crucial role in the continuous development of mushroom cultivation skills. Books, online courses, and workshops provide valuable insights into advanced growing techniques and business strategies. Networking opportunities through local farming associations or online forums can also help growers share knowledge and experiences. By investing in both equipment and education, mushroom cultivators can not only enhance their production capabilities but also position themselves for long-term success in the growing market of specialty fungi.

Mushroom Millions: Fungi Fortunes from Small Spaces

Choosing the Right Mushroom Varieties

When selecting the right mushroom varieties for cultivation, it is essential to consider both market demand and growing conditions. Different mushrooms cater to distinct culinary and medicinal needs, making it crucial to identify which varieties align with your target audience. Gourmet mushrooms such as shiitake, oyster, and lion's mane are popular among chefs and food enthusiasts, often commanding higher prices in local markets and restaurants. Conversely, medicinal mushrooms like reishi and chaga have gained traction in the wellness community, appealing to consumers seeking natural health solutions. Understanding these market dynamics can guide your choices and enhance your profitability.

Growing conditions play a pivotal role in determining which mushroom varieties will thrive in your setup. Factors such as temperature, humidity, and substrate type significantly influence the success of your cultivation efforts.

Mushroom Millions: Fungi Fortunes from Small Spaces

For urban and suburban homesteaders with limited space, substrate options like coffee grounds or straw can be ideal for growing oyster mushrooms, which are known for their adaptability. Shiitake mushrooms, on the other hand, thrive on hardwood logs or sawdust and may require slightly more space and care. Assessing your environment and available resources will help you choose varieties that not only flourish but also suit your space constraints.

Another aspect to consider is the growth cycle and yield potential of various mushroom types. Fast-growing varieties, such as oyster mushrooms, can produce multiple flushes within a few weeks, making them suitable for quick returns on investment. In contrast, species like shiitake take longer to mature but may yield higher profits per unit due to their gourmet status. Balancing quick turnover with high-value crops can create a diversified portfolio that stabilizes income streams and reduces risk. Therefore, it's vital to analyze the growth rates and economic viability of each variety before making your final decision.

Mushroom Millions: Fungi Fortunes from Small Spaces

Sustainable practices are increasingly important in the mushroom farming industry, especially for entrepreneurs focused on eco-friendly solutions. Choosing organic mushroom varieties that can be cultivated with minimal environmental impact not only aligns with sustainable living principles but also appeals to a growing market segment that prioritizes organic certifications. Utilizing waste products as substrates, such as agricultural byproducts or recycled materials, can enhance the sustainability of your operation while reducing costs. This approach can position your business as a leader in the sustainable mushroom market, attracting customers who value environmentally responsible practices.

Finally, effective online marketing strategies can help you connect with your audience and promote the unique qualities of your chosen mushroom varieties. Building a brand around your mushroom cultivation efforts involves showcasing the distinct flavors, health benefits, and sustainability practices associated with your products. Engaging storytelling about your cultivation journey, recipes featuring your mushrooms, and their potential health benefits can create a loyal customer base.

www.farmers-library.com

Mushroom Millions: Fungi Fortunes from Small Spaces

By leveraging social media platforms, e-commerce sites, and local food networks, you can maximize your outreach and capitalize on the growing interest in specialty mushrooms. This strategic marketing approach, combined with thoughtful selection of mushroom varieties, can pave the way to success in the flourishing world of mushroom entrepreneurship.

Mushroom Millions: Fungi Fortunes from Small Spaces

Setting Up Your Growing Space

Creating an effective growing space for mushroom cultivation is essential for maximizing yield and ensuring a successful venture. Whether you are a small-scale farmer or an urban homesteader, understanding the specific requirements of different mushroom species is crucial. Start by assessing the available space you have—this could be a basement, a garage, or even a small corner of your backyard. Each of these areas can be tailored to create an optimal environment for growing mushrooms, taking into account factors such as temperature, humidity, and light.

Temperature regulation is one of the most critical aspects of setting up your growing space. Most gourmet and medicinal mushrooms thrive within specific temperature ranges, generally between 55°F to 75°F. Installing a thermometer and a hygrometer will help you monitor these conditions effectively. If your chosen space tends to fluctuate in temperature, consider investing in heaters or air conditioning units, along with insulation materials to maintain a stable environment. Additionally, creating zones within your space for different species can help cater to varying temperature needs.

Mushroom Millions: Fungi Fortunes from Small Spaces

Humidity plays a vital role in mushroom development, as most species require a high level of moisture to fruit properly. Using a humidifier can assist in maintaining the necessary humidity levels, while also ensuring good air circulation to prevent mold growth. For those with limited budgets, DIY humidity trays filled with water can be an effective alternative. Furthermore, incorporating a misting system can automate watering and maintain optimal moisture levels, allowing you to focus on other aspects of your mushroom business.

Lighting is another essential consideration, as mushrooms do not need direct sunlight but do benefit from indirect light to trigger fruiting. If your growing space lacks natural light, fluorescent or LED grow lights can be an effective substitute. It's important to establish a light schedule, generally providing around 12 hours of light followed by 12 hours of darkness, to mimic natural conditions. This will help stimulate growth and assist in producing a more robust yield, which is particularly important for those targeting gourmet mushrooms for local restaurants and chefs.

Mushroom Millions: Fungi Fortunes from Small Spaces

Finally, consider the layout and organization of your growing space, as this can greatly influence efficiency and ease of maintenance. Utilizing vertical farming solutions can maximize space, allowing for higher production rates in smaller areas. Shelving units or racks can help you stack growing containers, while also providing easy access for monitoring and harvesting. By carefully planning your growing space, you not only enhance your productivity but also create a visually appealing environment that can inspire others and showcase your commitment to sustainable practices in mushroom farming.

Mushroom Millions: Fungi Fortunes from Small Spaces

Chapter 3: Specialty Mushroom Varieties for Urban Farmers

Gourmet Mushrooms: A Culinary Delight

Gourmet mushrooms have emerged as a culinary sensation, captivating the attention of chefs and food enthusiasts alike. Varieties such as shiitake, oyster, lion's mane, and maitake not only offer unique flavors and textures but also elevate dishes to new heights. Their rich umami profiles make them a favorite among gourmet cooks, who utilize these fungi to enhance sauces, risottos, and even desserts. This growing interest presents a lucrative opportunity for small-scale farmers and urban growers to tap into a market that values high-quality, locally sourced ingredients.

For those interested in cultivating gourmet mushrooms, understanding the specific growing conditions is vital. These mushrooms thrive in controlled environments, making them ideal candidates for small-scale production in urban settings.

Mushroom Millions: Fungi Fortunes from Small Spaces

Factors such as temperature, humidity, and substrate composition play a crucial role in successful cultivation. By using innovative methods such as vertical farming or utilizing small spaces effectively, growers can optimize their yields and produce superior quality mushrooms that meet the standards of discerning chefs and restaurants.

Marketing gourmet mushrooms requires a strategic approach that highlights their unique qualities and health benefits. Educating potential customers about the culinary versatility and nutritional advantages of these fungi can foster a loyal consumer base. Using platforms like social media and local farmers' markets provides excellent avenues for reaching gourmet food enthusiasts and restaurant owners. Additionally, establishing partnerships with local chefs can enhance visibility and create demand for specialty mushroom varieties, further driving sales and profitability for growers.

Mushroom Millions: Fungi Fortunes from Small Spaces

Sustainable practices in mushroom farming not only appeal to environmentally conscious consumers but also enhance the overall quality of the product. Utilizing organic materials for substrate, implementing waste recycling methods, and adopting eco-friendly pest management techniques are all ways to align with sustainable principles. This commitment to sustainability can be a significant selling point, attracting customers who prioritize ethical sourcing and environmental stewardship in their purchasing decisions.

As interest in gourmet mushrooms continues to grow, so does the potential for innovation within this niche. Entrepreneurs can explore opportunities to develop DIY mushroom growing kits for home cultivation, catering to the rising trend of self-sufficiency and home gardening. By providing resources that empower consumers to grow their own gourmet mushrooms, businesses not only tap into a profitable market but also promote a deeper connection between people and their food. This multifaceted approach to gourmet mushroom cultivation and marketing offers a pathway to financial success while contributing positively to the local food landscape.

Mushroom Millions: Fungi Fortunes from Small Spaces

Medicinal Mushrooms: Health Benefits and Uses

Medicinal mushrooms have gained significant attention in recent years due to their potent health benefits and versatile applications. Varieties such as reishi, lion's mane, chaga, and cordyceps are celebrated not just for their culinary uses but also for their therapeutic properties. These fungi are rich in bioactive compounds, including polysaccharides, triterpenes, and antioxidants, which contribute to their ability to enhance the immune system, reduce inflammation, and provide mental clarity. For small-scale farmers and urban homesteaders, incorporating medicinal mushrooms into their cultivation practices can open new avenues for revenue generation and diversify their product offerings.

Reishi mushrooms, often referred to as the "mushroom of immortality," are known for their ability to promote relaxation and improve sleep quality. They have been used in traditional Chinese medicine for centuries and are particularly sought after for their potential to help manage stress and anxiety. Farmers focusing on wellness products can market reishi as a natural supplement in various forms, including teas, tinctures, and powders.

Mushroom Millions: Fungi Fortunes from Small Spaces

By cultivating reishi mushrooms, growers can tap into the expanding market for holistic health solutions, appealing to consumers seeking natural alternatives to pharmaceuticals.

Lion's mane mushrooms have garnered attention for their neuroprotective properties, which may support cognitive function and memory. These unique fungi contain compounds that stimulate nerve growth factor (NGF) production, making them a popular choice among wellness enthusiasts. Urban farmers can leverage the growing interest in brain health by incorporating lion's mane into their product lines. Offering fresh mushrooms, dried products, or value-added items like lion's mane coffee blends can attract health-conscious consumers and elevate the farm's visibility within the wellness community.

Chaga and cordyceps mushrooms also present lucrative opportunities for cultivation and sales. Chaga, known for its high antioxidant content, is often used to support immune health and overall wellness. It can be marketed as a superfood supplement, appealing to those interested in preventive health measures.

Mushroom Millions: Fungi Fortunes from Small Spaces

On the other hand, cordyceps are prized for their energy-boosting properties, making them popular among athletes and fitness enthusiasts. By emphasizing these unique benefits, growers can position their mushrooms as essential components of a healthy lifestyle, tapping into the thriving market for functional foods.

In conclusion, the rise of medicinal mushrooms presents an exciting opportunity for small-scale farmers and urban homesteaders. With their remarkable health benefits and increasing consumer demand for natural health products, cultivating these specialty mushrooms can lead to profitable ventures. By integrating educational marketing strategies and sustainable farming practices, growers can successfully navigate this niche market, contributing to both their economic success and the well-being of their communities. Embracing the potential of medicinal mushrooms not only enhances the diversity of farm offerings but also aligns with the growing trend toward holistic and sustainable living.

Mushroom Millions: Fungi Fortunes from Small Spaces

Exotic Varieties: Expanding Your Offerings

Exotic varieties of mushrooms present a unique opportunity for growers seeking to diversify their offerings and tap into niche markets. While popular varieties like white button and portobello mushrooms dominate the market, exotic species such as lion's mane, shiitake, and maitake can capture the interest of gourmet chefs, health-conscious consumers, and food enthusiasts. Introducing these specialty mushrooms not only enhances your product line but also positions you as a supplier of unique culinary experiences and health benefits, appealing to a broader customer base.

Growing exotic mushrooms often requires different cultivation techniques and environmental conditions compared to standard varieties. For instance, lion's mane mushrooms thrive in slightly cooler temperatures and prefer hardwood substrates, making them a perfect candidate for small-scale, indoor farms or urban settings. Understanding the specific needs of each exotic variety is crucial for successful cultivation. By leveraging the knowledge of their growth requirements, you can optimize your growing conditions and yield high-quality products that stand out in the marketplace.

Mushroom Millions: Fungi Fortunes from Small Spaces

Marketing exotic mushrooms involves educating consumers about their culinary uses and health benefits. These mushrooms often contain unique flavors and textures that can enhance a wide range of dishes, from gourmet restaurant fare to home-cooked meals. Furthermore, many exotic varieties are touted for their potential medicinal properties, such as boosting cognitive function or supporting immune health. By creating engaging content that highlights these aspects—through blogs, social media posts, or cooking demonstrations—you can effectively reach your target audience and encourage them to try your products.

Incorporating exotic mushrooms into your offerings can also enhance your brand's reputation and sustainability profile. Many consumers today prioritize products that are not only flavorful but also sustainably sourced. By practicing organic farming techniques and promoting the ecological benefits of mushroom cultivation—such as their role in carbon sequestration and soil health—you can attract environmentally conscious consumers.

Mushroom Millions: Fungi Fortunes from Small Spaces

This alignment with sustainable practices not only meets customer demand but can also lead to partnerships with local restaurants and health food stores looking to source responsibly grown ingredients.

Expanding your mushroom offerings with exotic varieties is not just about increasing sales; it's an opportunity to build a community of mushroom enthusiasts. Hosting workshops or farm tours can foster connections with local consumers and fellow growers, allowing for the exchange of ideas and experiences. Additionally, participating in farmers' markets or specialty food festivals can provide valuable exposure and direct feedback from customers. By cultivating these relationships, you can create a loyal customer base that values your unique contributions to the mushroom industry, enhancing your success as a small-scale producer in a competitive market.

Mushroom Millions: Fungi Fortunes from Small Spaces

Chapter 4: DIY Mushroom Growing Kits for Small Spaces

Designing Your Own Kits

Designing your own mushroom growing kits can be an exciting and profitable venture for small-scale farmers and urban homesteaders. By creating specialized kits, you not only cater to a growing market for gourmet and medicinal mushrooms but also empower others to grow their own food sustainably. The first step in designing your kit is to choose the right mushroom varieties that appeal to your target audience. Whether it's the culinary delights of shiitake and oyster mushrooms or the health benefits of reishi and lion's mane, understanding the preferences of your potential customers is crucial.

Next, consider the components of your kit. A successful mushroom growing kit typically includes a substrate, spawn, and detailed instructions. The substrate serves as the foundation for growth and can range from sawdust to straw, depending on the mushroom variety.

Mushroom Millions: Fungi Fortunes from Small Spaces

Selecting organic and locally sourced materials not only enhances the quality of your mushrooms but also aligns with sustainable practices that resonate with your audience. Providing high-quality spawn is equally important, as it influences the yield and health of the mushrooms. Partnering with reputable spawn suppliers ensures that your kits will produce thriving fungi.

The packaging of your kit plays a significant role in attracting customers. Eye-catching designs that communicate the benefits of growing mushrooms, along with clear instructions, can make your product stand out in a crowded marketplace. Consider eco-friendly packaging options that highlight your commitment to sustainability. Including additional resources, such as online support or access to a community forum, can enhance the value of your kit and foster customer loyalty. Remember, the more engaging and informative your packaging, the more likely customers will be to choose your product over competitors.

Mushroom Millions: Fungi Fortunes from Small Spaces

Marketing your DIY mushroom growing kits effectively is key to reaching your audience. Utilize online platforms to showcase your products, sharing tutorials and success stories that inspire potential customers. Social media can be particularly powerful, allowing you to create a community around your brand. Collaborating with food and wellness influencers can also extend your reach and lend credibility to your offerings. Additionally, consider local farmers' markets or urban gardening events as venues for direct sales and engagement with your target demographic.

Finally, continuous improvement is vital for long-term success in this niche. Gather feedback from customers to refine your kits based on their experiences. Experiment with different varieties and substrates, staying informed about trends in the mushroom market. By adapting to the evolving needs and interests of your audience, you can ensure that your mushroom growing kits remain relevant and profitable. Designing your own kits not only provides a pathway to financial success but also promotes sustainable living and the joy of home cultivation.

Mushroom Millions: Fungi Fortunes from Small Spaces

Sourcing Materials and Supplies

Sourcing materials and supplies for mushroom cultivation is a critical step that can significantly influence the success of your venture. As a grower, understanding the essential inputs required for optimal mushroom production is vital. These materials can range from substrates and spawn to tools and equipment. Identifying reliable suppliers who can provide high-quality, organic materials is essential for maintaining the integrity of your cultivation process. Start by researching local agricultural suppliers, online marketplaces, and specialty mushroom vendors that focus on sustainable practices. Building strong relationships with these suppliers can lead to better pricing, availability, and support.

The substrate is one of the most important components in mushroom cultivation. Common substrates include straw, sawdust, coffee grounds, and wood chips, each offering unique benefits for different mushroom varieties. For example, oyster mushrooms thrive on straw, whereas shiitake mushrooms prefer hardwood sawdust. It's important to select substrates that are readily available in your area to minimize costs and transportation efforts.

Mushroom Millions: Fungi Fortunes from Small Spaces

Additionally, consider incorporating waste products from local industries, such as spent brewery grains or agricultural residues, which can create a sustainable loop and reduce your environmental footprint.

Spawn is another crucial element that directly affects your yield. Quality mushroom spawn can be sourced from established suppliers who specialize in producing mycelium cultures. When searching for spawn, prioritize suppliers that focus on organic and non-GMO practices. This ensures that you are cultivating mushrooms that are not only healthier but also more appealing to consumers who prioritize organic products. Take time to read reviews and seek recommendations from other growers to find reputable spawn suppliers. Some growers even opt to create their own spawn from high-quality cultures, allowing greater control over the cultivation process.

In addition to substrates and spawn, you'll need various tools and equipment tailored to your growing methods. Depending on your chosen cultivation style —be it indoor, outdoor, or vertical farming—your equipment needs may vary. Essential tools include sterile containers, humidity controllers, and temperature monitoring devices.

Mushroom Millions: Fungi Fortunes from Small Spaces

For those engaged in large-scale operations, investing in automated systems may be beneficial. However, for small-scale or urban growers, simple and cost-effective tools can suffice. Always consider the scale of your operation and choose equipment that balances functionality with your budget constraints.

Lastly, marketing your mushrooms is as important as sourcing your materials. Develop a strategy that highlights the unique qualities of your products, such as organic certification or specialty varieties. Utilize online platforms, social media, and local farmers' markets to reach potential customers. Networking with local restaurants and wellness entrepreneurs can also open doors for direct sales opportunities. By effectively sourcing your materials and supplies while simultaneously crafting a strong marketing strategy, you can build a successful mushroom business that thrives in the competitive market landscape.

Mushroom Millions: Fungi Fortunes from Small Spaces

Step-by-Step Kit Assembly

To successfully cultivate mushrooms at home, assembling a mushroom growing kit requires careful attention to detail and an understanding of the components involved. First, gather all necessary materials: a suitable container, sterile substrate, mushroom spawn, and any additional tools such as a spray bottle or thermometer. The container should be large enough to accommodate the chosen mushroom variety, with adequate ventilation to prevent excessive moisture buildup. Sterilizing the substrate is crucial, as it eliminates competing organisms that could hinder mushroom growth.

Once the materials are prepared, begin by layering the substrate in the container. This substrate, often composed of straw, sawdust, or coffee grounds, serves as the primary nourishment for the mushrooms. Aim for a thickness of approximately four to six inches, ensuring even distribution across the bottom of the container. After layering, create small holes or channels in the substrate where the mushroom spawn will be inserted. This step is essential, as it allows the spawn to spread and colonize the substrate effectively.

Mushroom Millions: Fungi Fortunes from Small Spaces

Next, introduce the mushroom spawn into the prepared substrate. This can be done by crumbling the spawn into small pieces and evenly distributing it throughout the substrate. Ensure that the spawn is thoroughly mixed in, which promotes optimal colonization. Once the spawn is added, cover the container with a breathable material, such as a cloth or plastic wrap with small holes, to maintain humidity while allowing for gas exchange. This balance is vital for the growth process, as mushrooms thrive in a humid environment with fresh airflow.

After assembling the kit, place it in a suitable location that offers the right temperature and light conditions for the specific mushroom variety being grown. Most mushrooms prefer temperatures between 60°F and 75°F, depending on the species. It's essential to monitor environmental conditions regularly, adjusting the placement of the kit as necessary to maintain ideal growing conditions. Light should be indirect; mushrooms do not require intense sunlight, but they do benefit from some exposure to natural light.

Mushroom Millions: Fungi Fortunes from Small Spaces

Finally, maintaining the kit involves regular watering and monitoring for contamination. Use a spray bottle to mist the substrate lightly, ensuring it remains moist but not overly saturated. Check for signs of mold or other unwanted organisms, as these can jeopardize your mushroom crop. With consistent care and attention, your mushroom growing kit will thrive, leading to a bountiful harvest that can be enjoyed personally or sold for profit, aligning perfectly with your goals as a sustainable living enthusiast or entrepreneur in the mushroom industry.

Chapter 5: Organic Mushroom Farming Techniques

Soil and Substrate Preparation

Soil and substrate preparation is a critical step in successful mushroom cultivation, serving as the foundation for healthy growth and abundant yields. Unlike traditional crops, mushrooms do not grow in soil but require a carefully prepared substrate, which can be composed of various organic materials. Common substrates include straw, sawdust, coffee grounds, and agricultural waste. Each type offers different benefits and challenges, making it essential for growers to understand the characteristics of these materials before embarking on their mushroom cultivation journey.

The first step in substrate preparation is selecting the appropriate material based on the mushroom species being cultivated. For instance, oyster mushrooms thrive on straw and sawdust, while shiitake mushrooms prefer hardwood sawdust or logs.

Mushroom Millions: Fungi Fortunes from Small Spaces

Once the substrate is chosen, it must be pasteurized or sterilized to eliminate competing microorganisms that could jeopardize the growth of the desired fungi. This can be achieved through methods such as steaming, boiling, or using a pressure cooker, ensuring that the substrate is free from contaminants that might hinder successful colonization by mushroom spores.

After pasteurization or sterilization, the substrate needs to be cooled to a temperature that is suitable for inoculation. This is a crucial step because introducing mushroom spores or spawn at elevated temperatures can kill them. Once the substrate reaches room temperature, it can be inoculated with the chosen mushroom spawn. It's important to maintain a clean and sterile environment during this process to prevent contamination. Using gloves and working in a sanitized area can significantly reduce the chances of unwanted bacteria or mold taking root in the substrate.

Mushroom Millions: Fungi Fortunes from Small Spaces

Post-inoculation, the substrate should be placed in a suitable container, such as plastic bags, jars, or trays, depending on the cultivation method chosen. The containers must provide adequate ventilation while also retaining moisture, as mushrooms require a humid environment to flourish. Monitoring the moisture content is vital; if the substrate becomes too dry, it can inhibit growth, while excessive moisture can lead to rot or mold. Regular checks and adjustments can help maintain the ideal conditions for the mycelium to colonize the substrate thoroughly.

Finally, once the mycelium has fully colonized the substrate, it is ready for fruiting. This stage involves creating the right environmental conditions, including temperature, humidity, and light exposure, to encourage the mushrooms to emerge. Understanding the specific needs of different mushroom varieties during this phase can lead to successful fruiting and a bountiful harvest. By mastering soil and substrate preparation, growers can set the stage for not only successful mushroom cultivation but also a profitable venture, tapping into the growing market for gourmet and medicinal mushrooms.

Mushroom Millions: Fungi Fortunes from Small Spaces

Pest and Disease Management

Pest and disease management is a crucial aspect of mushroom cultivation that significantly impacts both yield and quality. For growers operating in small spaces, whether urban or suburban, understanding the common threats to mushroom health is essential. Pests such as fruit flies, mites, and fungus gnats can invade your growing environment, competing for resources and directly damaging your crop. Diseases like bacterial blotch, cobweb mold, and trichoderma can also pose significant risks. Implementing integrated pest management (IPM) strategies can help mitigate these threats while promoting a healthy growing ecosystem.

Preventative measures are the first line of defense in pest and disease management. Maintaining cleanliness in your growing area is vital. This includes regular sanitation of tools, containers, and surfaces to eliminate potential breeding grounds for pests. Additionally, controlling humidity and temperature within the growing space can deter pests and prevent the onset of diseases. Monitoring your crops closely for any signs of stress or infestation can enable early detection and intervention, which is key to preventing larger outbreaks.

Mushroom Millions: Fungi Fortunes from Small Spaces

Biological controls offer an eco-friendly approach to managing pests and diseases. For instance, introducing beneficial microorganisms can help suppress harmful pathogens in the substrate. Certain fungi and bacteria can outcompete or inhibit the growth of undesirable species, promoting a balanced microbial environment. Similarly, using nematodes or predatory mites can help control pest populations without resorting to chemical pesticides, aligning with sustainable practices favored by many small-scale and urban growers.

When it comes to dealing with an active infestation or disease outbreak, quick action is necessary. Quarantine affected crops to prevent the spread of disease to healthy plants. Depending on the situation, options may include removing and destroying infected material or applying organic treatments like neem oil or garlic sprays. For fungal diseases, it may be beneficial to adjust environmental conditions, such as reducing humidity or improving air circulation, to create less favorable conditions for pathogens.

Mushroom Millions: Fungi Fortunes from Small Spaces

Finally, education and continuous learning are pivotal in effective pest and disease management. Growers should invest time in researching best practices, attending workshops, and joining online forums where they can share experiences and solutions with fellow mushroom cultivators. By fostering a community of knowledge and support, you can stay ahead of potential threats and ensure the success and sustainability of your mushroom venture. The right pest and disease management strategies will not only protect your investment but also enhance the quality of your gourmet or medicinal mushrooms, ultimately leading to greater profits and satisfaction.

Mushroom Millions: Fungi Fortunes from Small Spaces

Sustainable Practices in Organic Farming

Sustainable practices in organic farming play a crucial role in the successful cultivation of mushrooms, particularly as interest in gourmet and medicinal varieties grows. Organic mushroom farming emphasizes a holistic approach that enhances soil health, promotes biodiversity, and minimizes environmental impact. By employing sustainable methods, growers can create a thriving ecosystem that not only produces high-quality fungi but also contributes positively to the community and the planet.

One of the foundational sustainable practices in organic mushroom farming is the use of organic substrates. Farmers can utilize agricultural byproducts such as straw, coffee grounds, and sawdust, which are often considered waste. This practice not only reduces reliance on synthetic materials but also recycles resources that would otherwise contribute to landfill waste.

By transforming these byproducts into nutrient-rich substrates, mushroom growers can enhance their yield while promoting a circular economy.

Mushroom Millions: Fungi Fortunes from Small Spaces

Crop rotation and companion planting are additional methods that support sustainable mushroom farming. Implementing diverse crop rotations can help prevent soil depletion and disrupt pest cycles, reducing the need for chemical interventions. Companion planting, where mushrooms are grown alongside compatible plants, can enhance soil fertility and create a more resilient ecosystem. For instance, certain plants may attract beneficial insects or enhance the growth conditions for mushrooms, fostering a natural balance in the farming environment.

Water conservation is another vital aspect of sustainable organic mushroom farming. Growers can implement efficient irrigation systems, such as drip irrigation, to minimize water waste. Additionally, rainwater harvesting can provide a sustainable water source for cultivation. By utilizing these practices, farmers not only conserve a precious resource but also reduce operational costs, which is particularly beneficial for small-scale and urban growers.

Mushroom Millions: Fungi Fortunes from Small Spaces

Lastly, education and community engagement are essential components of sustainable practices in organic mushroom farming. By sharing knowledge and resources, growers can foster a supportive community that prioritizes sustainability and innovation. Workshops, local farmer markets, and online platforms can facilitate the exchange of ideas and best practices, empowering individuals to adopt sustainable methods in their own mushroom cultivation efforts. This collaborative spirit not only enhances the success of mushroom farming but also contributes to broader environmental stewardship and sustainable living initiatives.

Chapter 6: Vertical Farming Solutions for Mushroom Production

Understanding Vertical Farming Concepts

Vertical farming represents a revolutionary approach to agriculture that maximizes space and resources while minimizing environmental impact. This method involves growing crops in stacked layers or vertically inclined surfaces, which is particularly beneficial in urban settings where land is limited. For mushroom cultivation, vertical farming offers a unique opportunity to optimize production by using controlled environments that can significantly enhance growth rates and yields. By leveraging technology, growers can create ideal conditions for various mushroom species, ensuring consistent quality and availability throughout the year.

One of the key concepts in vertical farming is the use of hydroponic and aeroponic systems, which can be adapted for mushrooms.

Mushroom Millions: Fungi Fortunes from Small Spaces

While traditional mushroom cultivation relies on substrate for growth, integrating these techniques allows for innovative approaches to nutrient delivery and moisture control. This not only saves space but also reduces the need for extensive soil management, making it easier for small-scale farmers and urban homesteaders to engage in mushroom production. As these systems become more affordable and accessible, more individuals can explore the potential of vertical farming for fungi.

Sustainability is a core principle of vertical farming, aligning perfectly with the goals of environmentally conscious growers. This method utilizes significantly less water than conventional farming, as water can be recycled within the system. Additionally, vertical farms can be designed to run on renewable energy sources, further reducing their carbon footprint. Mushroom cultivation, particularly with specialty varieties, can thrive in such systems, promoting the growth of gourmet and medicinal mushrooms that cater to the increasing demand for organic and health-focused products. This sustainability aspect not only appeals to consumers but also enhances the marketability of the products.

Mushroom Millions: Fungi Fortunes from Small Spaces

The economic viability of vertical farming for mushrooms is particularly promising. With the ability to produce high-value crops in smaller spaces, growers can tap into lucrative markets, including local restaurants and specialty grocery stores. This method allows for year-round production, reducing the reliance on seasonal crops and enabling a steady stream of income. Additionally, by using online marketing strategies, mushroom entrepreneurs can effectively reach a broader audience, showcasing their unique offerings and cultivating a loyal customer base dedicated to sustainable eating.

In conclusion, understanding the concepts of vertical farming opens new avenues for mushroom cultivation, especially for those interested in small-scale and sustainable practices. As technology and techniques continue to evolve, the potential for profitability and environmental stewardship becomes increasingly apparent. By adopting vertical farming methods, growers can not only maximize their production capabilities but also contribute to a more sustainable food system, ultimately ensuring a thriving business model that aligns with the values of today's consumers.

Mushroom Millions: Fungi Fortunes from Small Spaces

Designing Vertical Systems for Mushrooms

Designing vertical systems for mushrooms is an innovative approach that maximizes space and enhances productivity. With the growing interest in urban farming and sustainable living, vertical cultivation methods offer an efficient way to produce mushrooms in limited spaces. Utilizing shelving units or stacked containers allows growers to take advantage of vertical height, which is particularly beneficial for small-scale farmers and homesteaders looking to optimize their available area. This method not only increases yield per square foot but also enables year-round production, catering to the increasing demand for fresh and specialty mushrooms.

When planning a vertical mushroom farm, it is essential to consider the types of mushrooms best suited for this system. Species like oyster and shiitake mushrooms thrive in controlled environments and can be successfully grown in stacked configurations. Each tier of the vertical system can be tailored to specific humidity and temperature requirements, allowing for a diverse range of mushroom varieties to be cultivated simultaneously.

Mushroom Millions: Fungi Fortunes from Small Spaces

This flexibility is ideal for side hustle entrepreneurs who wish to experiment with different gourmet and medicinal mushrooms while maximizing their market reach.

The design of the vertical system should prioritize accessibility and airflow. Proper spacing between tiers is crucial to ensure that air circulation is sufficient, preventing the buildup of moisture that can lead to mold and diseases. Additionally, incorporating features such as adjustable shelving and removable trays can facilitate easier harvesting and maintenance. For urban and suburban homesteaders, ease of use is paramount; therefore, systems that allow for straightforward assembly and disassembly can be particularly appealing, enabling growers to adapt their setups based on seasonal changes or product availability.

Sustainability is a core principle in modern mushroom farming, and vertical systems can be designed with eco-friendly practices in mind. Using recycled materials for construction, such as repurposed wood or plastic, can significantly reduce the environmental footprint.

Mushroom Millions: Fungi Fortunes from Small Spaces

Furthermore, implementing a nutrient-rich substrate from local agricultural waste not only supports sustainable practices but can also lower production costs. By creating an efficient and environmentally friendly vertical farming operation, growers can attract food and wellness entrepreneurs who value sustainability in their sourcing.

Marketing and distribution strategies play a vital role in the success of vertical mushroom farming ventures. Building an online presence through social media, local farmers' markets, and partnerships with restaurants can enhance visibility and create a loyal customer base. Highlighting the unique aspects of the vertical system, such as its sustainability and the freshness of the produce, can differentiate products in a competitive marketplace. For those involved in the mushroom industry, understanding how to effectively communicate the benefits of vertically grown mushrooms can significantly influence consumer preferences and drive sales.

Mushroom Millions: Fungi Fortunes from Small Spaces

Benefits of Vertical Farming in Urban Settings

Vertical farming in urban settings offers a transformative approach to food production, particularly for mushroom cultivation. One of the primary benefits is the efficient use of space. Urban areas often face land scarcity, making traditional farming methods impractical. Vertical farms utilize vertical space to maximize yield, allowing growers to produce mushrooms in stacked layers. This method not only conserves land but also enables urban growers to cultivate a variety of specialty mushrooms, catering to local markets and restaurants that demand fresh, high-quality produce.

Another significant advantage of vertical farming is its potential for resource efficiency. These systems often incorporate hydroponics or other soil-less growing techniques, which can drastically reduce water usage compared to conventional farming. Additionally, vertical farms can be equipped with advanced climate control systems, allowing for year-round cultivation.

Mushroom Millions: Fungi Fortunes from Small Spaces

This consistent production cycle can lead to increased profitability for small-scale farmers and entrepreneurs, as they can meet year-round demand for gourmet and medicinal mushrooms without the seasonal constraints faced by traditional agricultural practices.

Sustainability is a core principle of vertical farming, aligning perfectly with the values of sustainable living enthusiasts and food entrepreneurs. By reducing transportation needs—since produce can be grown closer to where it is consumed—vertical farms decrease carbon footprints associated with food distribution. Furthermore, the integration of renewable energy sources, such as solar panels, can further enhance sustainability. This model not only supports the environment but also appeals to consumers who prioritize eco-friendly practices in their purchasing decisions, thus creating a loyal customer base for mushroom growers.

Mushroom Millions: Fungi Fortunes from Small Spaces

Vertical farming also encourages innovation and community engagement. Urban mushroom growers can leverage technology, such as automated growing systems and data analytics, to optimize production processes. This creates opportunities for collaboration among local entrepreneurs, fostering a community of innovators who share resources, knowledge, and marketing strategies. By establishing a network of urban farmers, growers can enhance their visibility and reach, tapping into niche markets for specialty mushrooms and capitalizing on the growing interest in locally sourced, organic produce.

Finally, vertical farming can play a crucial role in promoting food security within urban areas. As cities expand and populations grow, the demand for fresh, nutritious food increases. Vertical farms can provide a reliable source of mushrooms, which are not only versatile and delicious but also packed with health benefits. By focusing on cultivating medicinal varieties, urban growers can contribute to community wellness while also exploring lucrative markets. As more individuals turn to entrepreneurship in the food sector, the potential for vertical farming in urban settings continues to grow, paving the way for a sustainable and profitable future in mushroom cultivation.

Chapter 7: Gourmet Mushrooms for Restaurants and Chefs

Identifying Market Opportunities

Identifying market opportunities in the mushroom industry requires a keen understanding of current trends, consumer preferences, and the unique benefits that mushrooms offer. As the demand for sustainable and locally sourced food continues to rise, mushrooms stand out not only for their culinary versatility but also for their health benefits. This presents a significant opportunity for global growers, small-scale farmers, and urban homesteaders to tap into a market that values organic and specialty products. By focusing on gourmet varieties, medicinal applications, and sustainable practices, entrepreneurs can carve out a niche that caters to both local consumers and larger markets.

One promising avenue is the growing interest in gourmet mushrooms among chefs and restaurants seeking to elevate their menus. Specialty varieties like lion's mane, oyster, and shiitake are becoming increasingly popular due to their unique flavors and textures.

Mushroom Millions: Fungi Fortunes from Small Spaces

Small-scale farmers can leverage this trend by establishing direct relationships with local culinary professionals. By offering fresh, high-quality mushrooms, farmers can not only secure a steady income but also foster a community around their products. Participating in farmers' markets and food festivals can further enhance visibility and create opportunities for collaboration with chefs looking to innovate their offerings.

The rise of health consciousness among consumers has also opened doors for those interested in medicinal mushrooms. Varieties such as reishi, cordyceps, and turkey tail are gaining recognition for their potential health benefits, including immune support and stress reduction. Entrepreneurs can explore this market by creating educational content that informs consumers about the benefits of these mushrooms and developing products that incorporate them, such as teas, supplements, or functional foods. By positioning themselves as knowledgeable providers in the medicinal mushroom space, growers can attract health-focused customers and establish a loyal following.

Mushroom Millions: Fungi Fortunes from Small Spaces

Urban and suburban homesteaders have a unique advantage in mushroom cultivation due to the adaptability of these fungi to small spaces. DIY mushroom growing kits are becoming increasingly popular for those looking to engage in home cultivation. These kits can be marketed not only for personal use but also as gifts, tapping into the trend of experiential and sustainable living. Providing clear instructions and support for beginners can enhance the customer experience and encourage repeat purchases as they expand their home-growing endeavors.

Finally, effective online marketing strategies are essential for mushroom entrepreneurs to succeed in a competitive landscape. Utilizing social media platforms to showcase the cultivation process, share recipes, and educate consumers about the benefits of mushrooms can create a strong online presence. E-commerce solutions can facilitate sales of fresh mushrooms, growing kits, and related products, while also allowing for the expansion of customer reach beyond local markets. By embracing digital marketing, entrepreneurs can transform their passion for mushrooms into a thriving business that resonates with today's conscious consumers.

Mushroom Millions: Fungi Fortunes from Small Spaces

Building Relationships with Local Restaurants

Building relationships with local restaurants is a pivotal strategy for mushroom growers seeking to expand their market presence and generate consistent sales. Restaurants often prioritize fresh, local ingredients, and establishing a connection with chefs and restaurant owners can lead to mutually beneficial partnerships. By demonstrating the unique qualities of specialty mushrooms, local growers can position themselves as valuable suppliers, helping restaurants differentiate their menus and enhance their culinary offerings.

The first step in cultivating these relationships is understanding the needs and preferences of local restaurants. Chefs are often looking for unique ingredients that can elevate their dishes, and specialty mushrooms offer a diverse range of flavors, textures, and nutritional profiles. Growers should conduct research on the dining scene in their area, identifying restaurants that emphasize farm-to-table practices or those that focus on innovative cuisine. This knowledge allows mushroom producers to tailor their pitch, showcasing varieties that align with the restaurant's culinary vision and customer base.

Mushroom Millions: Fungi Fortunes from Small Spaces

Networking is essential in the restaurant industry. Attending local food events, farmers' markets, and culinary festivals provides opportunities to meet chefs and restaurant owners in an informal setting. Bringing samples of your mushrooms can be a powerful way to demonstrate their quality and flavor. Additionally, offering to collaborate on special events, such as mushroom tasting nights or farm tours, can further solidify these relationships. By actively engaging with the community, growers can create a network of supporters who are eager to promote their products.

Beyond initial introductions, maintaining ongoing communication is crucial for sustaining these relationships. Establishing a regular delivery schedule and being responsive to feedback helps build trust with restaurant partners. Providing updates on seasonal availability, new varieties, and unique offerings keeps chefs informed and invested in your products. Furthermore, sharing insights on preparation techniques or recipe ideas can enhance the value you provide, positioning yourself not just as a supplier, but as a culinary ally.

Mushroom Millions: Fungi Fortunes from Small Spaces

Lastly, leveraging social media and online marketing can amplify the visibility of these partnerships. Highlighting collaborations with local restaurants through social media posts, blog articles, or newsletters can attract new customers and generate buzz around your mushrooms. Encouraging chefs to share their experiences using your products on their platforms can also expand your reach. By effectively marketing these relationships, mushroom growers can foster a sense of community, drawing attention to the benefits of local sourcing and the exceptional quality of their specialty mushrooms.

Pricing and Packaging Strategies

Pricing and packaging strategies play a crucial role in the success of any mushroom business, especially for those operating in niche markets. Understanding the value of your product is the first step in determining an effective pricing strategy. Factors such as production costs, market demand, and competitor pricing should all be considered. For small-scale farmers and urban growers, pricing should reflect not only the quality of the mushrooms but also the unique selling propositions that differentiate their products, such as organic certification, gourmet varieties, or local sourcing. Conducting market research to gauge what customers are willing to pay can provide valuable insights and help establish a competitive yet profitable price point.

When it comes to packaging, the choice can significantly impact a product's appeal and marketability. For mushroom entrepreneurs, selecting sustainable packaging materials aligns with the values of many consumers today, particularly those interested in sustainable living. Eco-friendly packaging options can enhance the perceived value of the product while reducing environmental impact.

Mushroom Millions: Fungi Fortunes from Small Spaces

Consideration should also be given to practical aspects such as moisture retention, shelf life, and visual appeal. Clear labeling that highlights the variety, origin, and benefits of the mushrooms can further entice customers and facilitate informed purchasing decisions.

The concept of bundling products is another effective pricing strategy that can boost sales. For example, creating DIY mushroom growing kits that include everything needed for home cultivation—spawn, substrate, and instructions—can appeal to urban homesteaders and side hustle entrepreneurs looking for convenient options. By offering bundles at a slightly discounted rate compared to purchasing items separately, growers can encourage larger sales and introduce customers to new mushroom varieties. This approach not only simplifies the buying process but also enhances customer satisfaction by providing a comprehensive solution.

Online marketing strategies also play a pivotal role in shaping pricing and packaging decisions. With the rise of e-commerce, having a robust online presence allows mushroom entrepreneurs to reach a broader audience.

Mushroom Millions: Fungi Fortunes from Small Spaces

Utilizing social media platforms, email marketing, and online marketplaces can help in promoting unique products and driving sales. Pricing strategies can be adjusted based on the feedback and buying patterns observed in online sales data. Moreover, attractive packaging that photographs well can enhance visibility and appeal in digital marketplaces, making it essential to invest in high-quality design and photography.

Ultimately, the interplay between pricing and packaging strategies can either make or break a mushroom business. Entrepreneurs must remain adaptable, continuously evaluating market trends and consumer preferences. By ensuring that pricing reflects the quality and uniqueness of their mushrooms while utilizing innovative packaging, growers can create a compelling brand that resonates with their target audience. This thoughtful approach not only maximizes revenue potential but also fosters a loyal customer base passionate about the benefits of mushrooms in various culinary and wellness applications.

Chapter 8: Medicinal Mushrooms and Their Commercial Potential

Overview of Medicinal Mushroom Varieties

Medicinal mushrooms are gaining recognition for their diverse health benefits and commercial potential. Varieties such as Reishi, Lion's Mane, and Chaga are at the forefront of this trend, each offering unique properties that appeal to health-conscious consumers and wellness entrepreneurs. Reishi is often lauded for its immune-boosting effects and stress-relieving qualities, making it a popular choice among those seeking natural remedies for anxiety and fatigue. Lion's Mane, on the other hand, is celebrated for its cognitive-enhancing benefits, attracting attention from individuals interested in improving memory and focus. Chaga, known for its high antioxidant content, is increasingly used in teas and supplements, appealing to the health and wellness market.

The cultivation of these medicinal varieties presents an exciting opportunity for small-scale farmers and urban homesteaders.

Mushroom Millions: Fungi Fortunes from Small Spaces

With the right growing conditions, including temperature, humidity, and substrate, individuals can successfully cultivate these mushrooms in limited spaces such as backyards, basements, or even small vertical farms. The shift towards local and organic produce is driving demand, making it a profitable venture for those willing to invest time and effort into mushroom farming. Additionally, the relatively low startup costs associated with mushroom cultivation make it accessible for side hustle entrepreneurs looking to diversify their income streams.

Incorporating sustainable practices into mushroom cultivation not only enhances environmental responsibility but also appeals to a growing demographic of eco-conscious consumers. Techniques such as utilizing waste materials like sawdust or coffee grounds as substrates can reduce costs while promoting a circular economy. Moreover, organic certification can add significant value to the produce, allowing small-scale farmers to command higher prices in the market. By focusing on sustainability, growers not only contribute positively to the environment but also position themselves strategically within the competitive mushroom market.

Mushroom Millions: Fungi Fortunes from Small Spaces

Marketing medicinal mushrooms effectively is crucial for success. An online presence, utilizing social media platforms and e-commerce websites, can help reach a wider audience and establish brand recognition. Educational content that informs consumers about the health benefits of different mushroom varieties can drive interest and sales. Collaborations with local restaurants and wellness shops can further enhance visibility and create mutually beneficial partnerships. By leveraging digital marketing strategies, entrepreneurs can capitalize on the growing trend of health and wellness products.

The future of medicinal mushrooms in the marketplace is promising, with increasing consumer awareness and demand for natural health solutions. As the industry evolves, opportunities for innovation and differentiation abound. Whether through unique product offerings, sustainable cultivation techniques, or strategic marketing approaches, those involved in medicinal mushroom farming can carve out a niche for themselves in this burgeoning sector. With the right knowledge and commitment, small-scale growers can not only thrive but also contribute to a healthier society through the power of fungi.

Mushroom Millions: Fungi Fortunes from Small Spaces

Market Trends and Consumer Demand

Market trends in mushroom cultivation reveal a growing interest among consumers in both specialty and gourmet varieties. As the culinary world increasingly embraces unique flavors and innovative dishes, chefs and home cooks alike are turning to mushrooms as versatile ingredients. Varieties such as shiitake, oyster, and lion's mane are gaining popularity, not only for their taste but also for their nutritional benefits. The rise of plant-based diets has further fueled this trend, as mushrooms serve as a satisfying alternative to traditional meat products, leading to increased consumer demand.

In addition to culinary uses, there is a significant surge in the awareness of the health benefits associated with medicinal mushrooms. Varieties such as reishi, chaga, and cordyceps are being marketed for their potential health benefits, including immune support and stress reduction. As consumers become more health-conscious and seek natural remedies, the market for medicinal mushrooms continues to expand. This trend presents a lucrative opportunity for small-scale farmers and entrepreneurs who can tap into the growing demand for wellness-oriented products.

Mushroom Millions: Fungi Fortunes from Small Spaces

Urban and suburban homesteaders are increasingly finding ways to incorporate mushroom cultivation into their sustainable living practices. With limited space, many are turning to innovative growing methods such as vertical farming and container gardening. These techniques not only maximize small areas but also promote a self-sufficient lifestyle. The accessibility of DIY mushroom growing kits has made it easier for newcomers to enter the market, creating a community of enthusiasts eager to learn and share their experiences. This grassroots movement is driving consumer interest in locally sourced and homegrown produce.

The online marketplace has become a vital platform for mushroom entrepreneurs. As consumers seek unique and artisanal products, businesses that leverage digital marketing strategies can effectively reach their target demographics. Utilizing social media, e-commerce platforms, and content marketing, mushroom growers can connect with consumers looking for specialty varieties and growing kits.

Mushroom Millions: Fungi Fortunes from Small Spaces

By showcasing their products' quality and sustainability, they can build a loyal customer base that values both the uniqueness of their offerings and their commitment to responsible farming practices.

Sustainability is at the forefront of consumer decision-making, particularly in the food sector. As awareness of environmental issues grows, consumers are increasingly prioritizing products that align with their values. Mushroom farming, especially when approached with organic techniques and sustainable practices, is well-positioned to meet this demand. By emphasizing environmentally friendly methods and the minimal ecological footprint of mushroom cultivation, producers can not only attract health-conscious consumers but also contribute positively to the broader conversation about sustainable agriculture. This alignment with consumer values can enhance brand loyalty and drive sales in an increasingly competitive market.

Mushroom Millions: Fungi Fortunes from Small Spaces

Regulations and Safety Considerations

Navigating the regulations surrounding mushroom cultivation is essential for anyone looking to turn their passion into profit. Different regions have varying laws concerning agricultural practices, food safety, and business operations. It's crucial for growers to familiarize themselves with local, state, and federal guidelines that impact mushroom farming. This includes obtaining necessary permits, adhering to zoning laws, and ensuring compliance with health department standards. Understanding these regulations not only helps avoid potential legal pitfalls but also enhances the credibility of your business in the eyes of consumers and partners.

Safety considerations are paramount when cultivating mushrooms, particularly for those who are new to the practice. Cultivating mushrooms involves specific risks, including contamination and exposure to harmful species. Proper sanitation and sterile techniques are vital in preventing the growth of unwanted molds and bacteria. Growers should invest in quality materials and maintain clean workspaces to minimize these risks.

Mushroom Millions: Fungi Fortunes from Small Spaces

Additionally, it's important to educate oneself on identifying edible versus toxic mushroom varieties, as this knowledge is essential for safe consumption and sales.

For urban and suburban homesteaders, space constraints pose unique challenges in mushroom cultivation. Implementing safety measures tailored to small spaces can help mitigate risks associated with confined environments. For instance, ensuring adequate ventilation is critical to prevent the buildup of humidity and the growth of pathogens. Utilizing vertical farming techniques can optimize space while also enhancing safety protocols. By adopting a well-structured approach to growing mushrooms in limited areas, enthusiasts can enjoy a rewarding experience without compromising their health or safety.

Sustainable practices in mushroom farming not only align with the values of many modern consumers but also contribute to overall safety. Organic growing methods reduce the reliance on chemical fertilizers and pesticides, creating a healthier product. By using sustainable substrates, such as agricultural waste or recycled materials, growers can minimize environmental impact while promoting food safety.

Chapter 9: Sustainable Practices in Mushroom Farming

Environmental Benefits of Mushroom Cultivation

This approach not only appeals to health-conscious consumers but also enhances the marketability of gourmet and medicinal mushrooms, tapping into the growing demand for organic products.

Finally, understanding the regulations and safety considerations is critical for effective online marketing strategies. Transparency in farming practices can build consumer trust and loyalty. Highlighting compliance with local regulations and emphasizing safety measures in marketing materials can differentiate your products in a crowded marketplace. Effective communication of these elements can entice chefs, health enthusiasts, and consumers, ultimately driving sales and reinforcing the value of your mushroom business in the competitive landscape. By prioritizing safety and regulatory compliance, growers can pave the way for a thriving and sustainable venture.

Mushroom Millions: Fungi Fortunes from Small Spaces

Mushroom cultivation offers numerous environmental benefits that make it an appealing endeavor for global growers and small-scale farmers alike. One of the most significant advantages is the ability of mushrooms to decompose organic waste. Through the process of breaking down agricultural byproducts, food scraps, and other organic materials, mushrooms contribute to reducing landfill waste. This not only helps mitigate the environmental impact of waste disposal but also creates a valuable resource for mushroom production, turning potential waste into a sustainable growing medium.

In addition to waste decomposition, mushrooms play a vital role in enhancing soil health. The mycelium, the vegetative part of fungi, improves soil structure and promotes nutrient cycling. By interacting with plant roots and aiding in the absorption of essential nutrients, mycelium helps to create a more fertile environment for crops. This symbiotic relationship can be particularly beneficial for urban and suburban homesteaders who are looking to improve the sustainability of their small gardens or community plots, ultimately leading to healthier produce and a more robust ecosystem.

Mushroom Millions: Fungi Fortunes from Small Spaces

Mushroom cultivation also offers a unique opportunity for carbon sequestration. Fungi have the capability to capture carbon dioxide from the atmosphere through their growth processes. By cultivating mushrooms, growers contribute to a natural form of carbon capture, which can help mitigate climate change impacts. This characteristic aligns well with the values of sustainable living enthusiasts and offers a compelling reason to integrate mushroom farming into broader climate action strategies.

Furthermore, the practice of mushroom farming encourages biodiversity. By introducing various mushroom species into cultivation systems, growers can help maintain and promote ecological balance. This is especially important in urban farming settings, where biodiversity often suffers due to habitat loss and pollution. Specialty mushroom varieties cultivated in small spaces can create a rich diversity of food sources, attracting beneficial insects and contributing to healthy ecosystems.

Mushroom Millions: Fungi Fortunes from Small Spaces

Lastly, the environmental benefits extend to water conservation. Mushroom cultivation typically requires less water compared to traditional agricultural crops, making it an excellent option for side hustle entrepreneurs and those operating in regions facing water scarcity. By adopting organic mushroom farming techniques, growers not only limit their water usage but also reduce the need for chemical fertilizers and pesticides, leading to cleaner water systems and a healthier environment overall. Thus, the integration of mushroom cultivation into various agricultural practices not only offers economic potential but also fosters a healthier planet for future generations.

Mushroom Millions: Fungi Fortunes from Small Spaces

Waste Reduction and Recycling Techniques

Waste reduction and recycling techniques are crucial for mushroom cultivation, especially for small-scale farmers and urban growers. By implementing effective practices, you can minimize waste and convert potential discards into valuable resources. One of the primary waste sources in mushroom farming is the substrate, typically composed of agricultural byproducts such as straw, sawdust, or coffee grounds. After the mushrooms have been harvested, instead of disposing of the spent substrate, you can compost it or use it to enrich garden soil. This not only reduces waste but also promotes healthier plant growth, creating a sustainable cycle within your growing ecosystem.

Another innovative approach to waste reduction involves integrating mushroom cultivation with other agricultural practices. For instance, utilizing spent substrate as a feedstock for livestock or incorporating fungi into aquaponics systems can enhance symbiotic relationships within your farm. By diversifying your operations, you not only minimize waste but also create additional income streams.

Mushroom Millions: Fungi Fortunes from Small Spaces

This holistic approach not only contributes to environmental sustainability but also fosters resilience in your farming practices, making your operation more adaptable to changing market demands.

Recycling techniques also extend to packaging and distribution. Many small-scale mushroom entrepreneurs often overlook the environmental impact of their packaging choices. Using biodegradable or reusable materials for packaging can significantly reduce waste. Implementing a return program for your packaging, where customers can return containers for reuse, encourages sustainability while also fostering customer loyalty. This practice aligns perfectly with the values of your target audience, who are increasingly aware of sustainability issues and prefer to support businesses that reflect these values.

Furthermore, incorporating a waste audit into your operational practices can help identify areas for improvement. Regularly assessing your waste production allows you to pinpoint inefficiencies and develop targeted strategies to address them.

Mushroom Millions: Fungi Fortunes from Small Spaces

By tracking what materials are being discarded and understanding their potential for recycling or repurposing, you can create a closed-loop system that not only reduces waste but also enhances productivity. This proactive approach ensures that your mushroom farming operation remains sustainable and profitable.

Finally, education plays a vital role in promoting waste reduction and recycling techniques among your community and customers. Hosting workshops or informational sessions on sustainable practices in mushroom farming can empower others to adopt similar methods. By sharing your knowledge and experiences, you contribute to a broader movement toward responsible and sustainable agriculture. Engaging your audience in discussions about waste reduction not only elevates your brand's reputation but also positions you as a leader in the sustainable farming community, fostering a sense of shared purpose and responsibility.

Mushroom Millions: Fungi Fortunes from Small Spaces

Community Engagement and Education

Community engagement and education play a pivotal role in the success of mushroom cultivation initiatives, particularly for those in urban and suburban settings. By fostering a sense of community, growers can share resources, knowledge, and experiences that enhance the overall understanding of mushroom farming. Engaging local residents through workshops, seminars, and hands-on demonstrations can spark interest and inspire new entrepreneurs to explore mushroom cultivation. These activities also create a platform for exchanging ideas and best practices, which is crucial for both beginners and experienced growers seeking to refine their techniques.

Local partnerships can significantly boost community engagement efforts. Collaborating with schools, community centers, and local businesses provides opportunities to reach a broader audience. For instance, organizing educational programs in schools can introduce students to the fascinating world of fungi, promoting interest in sustainable agricultural practices from a young age.

Mushroom Millions: Fungi Fortunes from Small Spaces

Similarly, partnering with restaurants can highlight the culinary potential of gourmet mushrooms, while also creating a market for local growers. Such collaborations not only enhance visibility for mushroom farming but also help in building a supportive network of consumers and producers dedicated to sustainable food practices.

Education is equally vital in ensuring that small-scale farmers and urban growers are equipped with the necessary skills to thrive. By offering workshops that cover topics such as organic farming techniques, specialty mushroom varieties, and vertical farming solutions, aspiring entrepreneurs can gain practical knowledge to kickstart their mushroom-growing ventures. Accessible resources, such as online tutorials and DIY mushroom growing kits, can further empower individuals to cultivate mushrooms even in limited spaces. This hands-on approach demystifies the process and encourages more people to consider mushroom cultivation as a viable side hustle or full-time endeavor.

Furthermore, educating the community about the medicinal potential of mushrooms can open new avenues for commercialization.

Mushroom Millions: Fungi Fortunes from Small Spaces

With the growing interest in health and wellness, workshops that focus on medicinal mushroom varieties can attract health-conscious individuals eager to learn about their benefits. This not only expands the market for mushroom products but also positions local growers as knowledgeable sources within the wellness community. By promoting the nutritional and therapeutic aspects of mushrooms, growers can tap into a lucrative niche that aligns with the increasing consumer demand for holistic health solutions.

Finally, utilizing digital platforms for community engagement and education can significantly enhance outreach efforts. Social media, blogs, and online courses serve as effective tools for sharing knowledge and connecting with a global audience. By leveraging online marketing strategies, mushroom entrepreneurs can showcase their products and expertise, attracting customers beyond their immediate communities. This digital presence is particularly beneficial for those looking to scale their operations or reach niche markets, such as gourmet chefs or specialty health food stores.

Mushroom Millions: Fungi Fortunes from Small Spaces

In summary, fostering community engagement and prioritizing education are essential for the sustainable growth of mushroom farming, providing both economic opportunities and a deeper appreciation for the role of fungi in our food systems.

Chapter 10: Online Marketing Strategies for Mushroom Entrepreneurs

Building Your Brand Online

Building your brand online is essential for anyone looking to thrive in the mushroom farming industry, particularly for those engaged in small-scale operations and side hustles. Establishing a strong online presence allows you to connect with a wider audience, share your knowledge, and promote your unique offerings. Start by creating a professional website that showcases your brand story, products, and services. Include high-quality images of your mushrooms, cultivation processes, and even engaging videos demonstrating the versatility of your products. A well-designed website serves as a hub for your business, enabling potential customers to learn about you and your offerings while establishing credibility in the marketplace.

Social media platforms play a crucial role in building your brand online. Utilize platforms such as Instagram, Facebook, and TikTok to share visually appealing content that highlights your mushroom varieties and cultivation techniques.

Mushroom Millions: Fungi Fortunes from Small Spaces

Regularly post updates about your growing processes, seasonal offerings, and any events you participate in, such as farmers' markets or workshops. Engaging with your audience through comments and messages fosters a sense of community and loyalty, which can lead to repeat customers and word-of-mouth referrals. Collaborate with influencers in the food, wellness, and sustainable living spaces to amplify your reach and gain new followers who are interested in your niche.

Content marketing is another powerful tool for establishing your brand as an authority in the mushroom industry. Start a blog on your website where you can share valuable information about mushroom cultivation, recipes, and the health benefits of various mushroom varieties. Consider creating downloadable guides or e-books that delve deeper into specific topics, such as organic mushroom farming techniques or the medicinal properties of mushrooms. By providing insightful content, you not only attract potential customers but also position yourself as a knowledgeable resource in the field, which can enhance your brand's reputation.

Mushroom Millions: Fungi Fortunes from Small Spaces

Search engine optimization (SEO) is vital for increasing visibility online. Research keywords related to your niche, such as "DIY mushroom growing kits" or "gourmet mushrooms for restaurants," and incorporate them into your website content, blog posts, and social media updates. This strategy helps improve your search engine rankings, making it easier for potential customers to find your business. Additionally, consider using local SEO techniques to target customers in your area, which is particularly beneficial for small-scale farmers and local entrepreneurs who depend on community support.

Finally, don't underestimate the power of email marketing in building lasting relationships with your audience. Create a mailing list and send out regular newsletters featuring updates about your farm, new product offerings, and exclusive promotions. Encourage sign-ups by offering a discount on the first purchase or a free guide on mushroom cultivation. An effective email marketing strategy can keep your brand top-of-mind for customers and drive repeat sales. By combining these online branding strategies, you can effectively grow your business and connect with a community of like-minded enthusiasts in the mushroom farming industry.

Mushroom Millions: Fungi Fortunes from Small Spaces

Social Media and Content Marketing

Social media has revolutionized the way small-scale farmers and urban homesteaders connect with their audiences, making it an essential tool for promoting mushroom cultivation. Platforms like Instagram, Facebook, and TikTok allow growers to share their journey, showcase their products, and engage with fellow enthusiasts. The visual nature of these platforms is particularly beneficial for mushroom entrepreneurs, as mushrooms come in a variety of shapes, sizes, and colors that can capture the attention of potential customers. By posting high-quality images and videos of their grow operations, unique mushroom varieties, and DIY kits, growers can create a compelling narrative that draws in followers and builds a loyal customer base.

Content marketing plays a key role in establishing authority and trust within the mushroom farming community. By creating informative blog posts, how-to guides, and educational videos, mushroom growers can share their expertise and provide value to their audience. Topics might include the benefits of specific mushroom varieties, sustainable farming practices, or tips for successful home cultivation.

Mushroom Millions: Fungi Fortunes from Small Spaces

This not only positions the grower as a knowledgeable resource but also helps to drive traffic to their website and online store. Consistent, valuable content can enhance brand visibility and encourage shares, ultimately reaching a wider audience interested in gourmet and medicinal mushrooms.

Engagement is another vital aspect of social media marketing. Responding to comments, participating in discussions, and sharing user-generated content can foster a sense of community among mushroom enthusiasts. Growers can encourage followers to share their own mushroom-growing experiences, creating an interactive platform where knowledge is exchanged, and relationships are built. Utilizing social media stories and live-streaming can also help to showcase day-to-day operations and behind-the-scenes activities, making the brand more relatable and trustworthy. This personal touch can lead to increased brand loyalty and customer retention.

Collaborations with food and wellness entrepreneurs can amplify the reach of mushroom-related content. By partnering with chefs, nutritionists, or wellness advocates, mushroom growers can tap into established audiences that value organic and specialty food products.

Mushroom Millions: Fungi Fortunes from Small Spaces

Collaborations might include joint cooking demonstrations, recipe sharing, or educational webinars on the health benefits of medicinal mushrooms. These partnerships not only enhance credibility but also introduce the grower's products to new potential customers who are already interested in sustainable and healthy living.

Finally, leveraging targeted advertising on social media platforms can significantly boost visibility for mushroom businesses. Utilizing demographic and interest-based targeting allows growers to reach specific audiences, such as gourmet chefs, health-conscious consumers, or urban farmers. Promoting seasonal products, special offers, and workshops can drive immediate sales and generate interest in upcoming offerings. By analyzing engagement and conversion metrics, mushroom entrepreneurs can refine their marketing strategies to ensure they effectively reach their desired audience, ultimately leading to increased sales and growth in their mushroom enterprise.

Mushroom Millions: Fungi Fortunes from Small Spaces

E-commerce Platforms for Selling Mushrooms

E-commerce has transformed the way mushrooms are marketed and sold, providing an accessible platform for growers and entrepreneurs to reach a broader audience. For small-scale farmers and urban cultivators, leveraging online marketplaces can significantly increase visibility and sales potential. Platforms such as Etsy, Amazon, and eBay offer user-friendly interfaces, allowing sellers to create storefronts and list specialty mushroom varieties, DIY mushroom growing kits, and even medicinal mushrooms. These platforms cater to a diverse consumer base, from home cooks seeking gourmet ingredients to wellness enthusiasts looking for the health benefits of mushrooms.

Setting up an online shop requires careful consideration of product presentation and marketing strategies. High-quality images and informative descriptions are essential for capturing the attention of potential buyers. For mushroom entrepreneurs, showcasing unique aspects such as organic farming techniques, specialty varieties, and sustainable practices can differentiate their products in a crowded market.

Mushroom Millions: Fungi Fortunes from Small Spaces

Additionally, sharing stories about the cultivation process and the benefits of mushrooms can create a connection with customers, fostering loyalty and encouraging repeat purchases.

Beyond traditional e-commerce platforms, social media channels have emerged as powerful tools for promoting mushroom sales. Platforms like Instagram and Facebook allow growers to engage directly with customers, sharing enticing visuals of their products and the behind-the-scenes processes of cultivation. Creating a robust online presence through regular updates, educational content, and interactive posts not only builds a community around the brand but also drives traffic to the e-commerce site. Influencer collaborations and targeted advertising can further enhance visibility, reaching niche markets interested in gourmet and medicinal mushrooms.

Subscription boxes and online farmers' markets are additional avenues for mushroom sales, appealing to consumers interested in sustainable and local products. By partnering with local producers or joining a subscription service, mushroom growers can offer curated kits that include a variety of mushrooms or growing supplies, promoting the farm-to-table concept.

Mushroom Millions: Fungi Fortunes from Small Spaces

This not only supports local economies but also taps into the growing demand for fresh, organic produce delivered directly to consumers' doors.

Finally, understanding the logistics of e-commerce is crucial for ensuring a successful online business. This includes managing inventory, shipping, and customer service. Implementing efficient order fulfillment systems and establishing reliable shipping methods are vital for providing a seamless experience for customers. E-commerce platforms often offer tools and resources to streamline these processes, making it easier for small-scale mushroom farmers to focus on what they do best—growing high-quality fungi while expanding their reach in the marketplace.

Chapter 11: Scaling Your Mushroom Business

Expanding Production Capacity

Expanding production capacity is a crucial step for growers looking to maximize their mushroom yields and profits. As demand for gourmet and medicinal mushrooms continues to rise, it is essential for producers to identify strategies for scaling their operations effectively. This involves not only increasing the physical space dedicated to mushroom cultivation but also optimizing existing resources to enhance productivity. By leveraging innovative techniques and technology, growers can expand their capacity without compromising on quality or sustainability.

One effective method for expanding production is the implementation of vertical farming techniques. By utilizing vertical space, growers can significantly increase their output without the need for additional land. This approach is particularly beneficial for urban and suburban homesteaders, who may have limited space available for traditional farming methods.

Mushroom Millions: Fungi Fortunes from Small Spaces

Vertical systems can be tailored to various mushroom species, allowing for a diverse range of products to be cultivated simultaneously. Moreover, these systems can be designed to be highly efficient, utilizing controlled environments that optimize growth conditions and reduce resource consumption.

Investing in advanced cultivation technologies can also play a pivotal role in expanding production capacity. Automated systems for monitoring temperature, humidity, and light can enhance the growing environment, leading to faster growth rates and higher yields. Additionally, employing techniques such as substrate pasteurization and sterilization can improve the quality and consistency of the mushrooms produced. For small-scale farmers and side hustle entrepreneurs, these technologies may seem initially daunting, but the long-term benefits can significantly outweigh the upfront costs, making them a worthwhile investment.

Collaboration with local chefs and restaurants can further enhance production capacity by creating a direct market for specialty mushrooms. By establishing partnerships, growers can gain insights into consumer preferences and trends, allowing them to adjust their production accordingly.

Mushroom Millions: Fungi Fortunes from Small Spaces

This not only helps in increasing sales but also in building a reputation within the culinary community, which can lead to increased demand for unique and high-quality mushroom varieties. Such collaborations can serve as a powerful marketing tool, showcasing the fresh, locally-sourced nature of the products.

Lastly, adopting sustainable practices in mushroom farming is essential for long-term success and expansion. As consumers become more environmentally conscious, they increasingly seek products that are grown sustainably. Utilizing organic materials for substrates, implementing waste recycling processes, and reducing energy consumption are all strategies that can enhance the ecological footprint of mushroom farming. By embracing sustainability, growers not only contribute to a healthier planet but also attract a customer base that values ethical practices. This holistic approach to expanding production capacity can lead to a thriving business that aligns with the values of modern consumers.

Mushroom Millions: Fungi Fortunes from Small Spaces

Diversifying Product Lines

Diversifying product lines is a strategic approach for growers and entrepreneurs looking to maximize their profitability and stability in the mushroom market. With the rising interest in gourmet and medicinal mushrooms, there is a significant opportunity for small-scale farmers and urban homesteaders to expand their offerings beyond traditional varieties. By exploring specialty mushrooms, value-added products, and even educational services, cultivators can tap into various consumer demands and trends, ensuring their businesses remain resilient against market fluctuations.

One avenue for diversification is the cultivation of specialty mushroom varieties that appeal to niche markets. Varieties such as lion's mane, oyster, shiitake, and maitake are gaining popularity not only for their culinary uses but also for their health benefits. By growing mushrooms that are less commonly found in grocery stores, home growers and small farmers can attract chefs and health-conscious consumers willing to pay a premium. Developing relationships with local restaurants and specialty food stores can create reliable channels for these unique products, enhancing brand visibility and customer loyalty.

Mushroom Millions: Fungi Fortunes from Small Spaces

In addition to fresh mushrooms, entrepreneurs can consider venturing into value-added products. Items such as dried mushrooms, mushroom powders, and gourmet mushroom kits for home cultivation can significantly increase profit margins. These products cater to different consumer segments, including home cooks looking for convenience and those interested in growing their own food. Additionally, offering subscription boxes that include a variety of fresh mushrooms, recipes, and growing tips can appeal to the growing trend of home cooking and sustainable living.

Educational initiatives also present a valuable opportunity for diversification. Workshops, online courses, and informational webinars on mushroom cultivation can attract aspiring growers and enthusiasts. By sharing expertise in organic farming techniques, sustainable practices, and the medicinal properties of mushrooms, businesses can establish themselves as leaders in the field while generating additional revenue streams. This not only enhances customer engagement but also fosters a community of informed consumers who can become loyal advocates for the brand.

Mushroom Millions: Fungi Fortunes from Small Spaces

Finally, effective online marketing strategies will be essential in promoting diversified product lines. Utilizing social media platforms, email marketing, and e-commerce websites can help cultivators reach a broader audience. High-quality content showcasing the benefits, uses, and stories behind different mushroom varieties can engage potential customers and drive sales. By leveraging digital tools, mushroom entrepreneurs can establish brand identity, educate their audience, and ultimately create a thriving business that adapts to the evolving marketplace.

Mushroom Millions: Fungi Fortunes from Small Spaces

Collaborations and Partnerships

Collaborations and partnerships play a crucial role in the success of mushroom cultivation, particularly for small-scale farmers and urban growers seeking to enhance their operations and expand their market reach. By joining forces with local businesses, community organizations, and educational institutions, mushroom cultivators can leverage shared resources, knowledge, and customer bases. These collaborations can take various forms, from joint marketing initiatives to shared research projects, all aimed at promoting sustainable practices and increasing the visibility of specialty mushroom varieties.

For small-scale farmers and urban homesteaders, forming partnerships with local restaurants and chefs can significantly boost sales while fostering a sense of community. Gourmet mushrooms, such as shiitake, oyster, and lion's mane, are increasingly sought after in culinary circles for their unique flavors and health benefits. By establishing direct relationships with these food professionals, growers can create tailored offerings that meet specific culinary needs, ensuring a steady demand for their products.

Mushroom Millions: Fungi Fortunes from Small Spaces

This not only enhances profitability but also allows growers to receive valuable feedback on their mushrooms, helping them refine their cultivation techniques.

In addition to culinary partnerships, collaborations with local health and wellness entrepreneurs can open up new avenues for marketing medicinal mushrooms. As the interest in natural health solutions grows, products featuring medicinal mushrooms are becoming more prevalent. By partnering with health food stores, wellness centers, and herbalists, mushroom cultivators can tap into this expanding market. These partnerships can also facilitate educational workshops and events that highlight the benefits of mushrooms, creating community engagement while promoting product sales.

Educational institutions present another valuable partnership opportunity for mushroom growers. Collaborating with universities and research organizations can lead to innovative practices and sustainable farming techniques that benefit both growers and the environment. Such partnerships can also promote outreach programs that educate the public about the ecological importance of fungi and their potential for food security.

Mushroom Millions: Fungi Fortunes from Small Spaces

By engaging with academic institutions, growers can gain access to research funding, internship programs, and a pipeline of new ideas that can enhance their business models.

Lastly, in the digital age, strategic partnerships with online marketing platforms and e-commerce businesses can significantly expand the reach of mushroom products. By collaborating with websites that focus on sustainable living, organic farming, and culinary arts, growers can tap into niche markets and attract customers who are looking for local, high-quality produce. Utilizing social media and online marketplaces can amplify the visibility of mushroom offerings and create a broader customer base, ultimately leading to increased sales and business growth. Through these collaborative efforts, mushroom growers can not only thrive in their ventures but also contribute to a more sustainable food system.

Chapter 12: Future Trends in Mushroom Farming

Innovations in Cultivation Techniques

Innovations in cultivation techniques are transforming the way mushrooms are grown, particularly for small-scale farmers and urban homesteaders. Advances in technology and sustainable practices have enabled growers to maximize yields while minimizing their environmental impact. Key innovations include the use of controlled environment agriculture (CEA), which allows for precise regulation of temperature, humidity, and light, creating optimal conditions for mushroom growth. By implementing CEA, growers can produce high-quality mushrooms year-round, regardless of external climate conditions, making it an attractive option for urban farmers looking to thrive in limited spaces.

Another significant innovation is the development of substrate alternatives that enhance the nutritional profile and growth rates of mushrooms. Traditional substrates like straw or sawdust are now being supplemented with agricultural by-products such as spent coffee grounds, rice bran, and even food waste.

Mushroom Millions: Fungi Fortunes from Small Spaces

These innovative substrates not only reduce costs for growers but also promote sustainability by repurposing materials that would otherwise contribute to landfill waste. This approach aligns well with the values of sustainable living enthusiasts who prioritize eco-friendly practices and resource efficiency.

Vertical farming solutions have also gained traction in the mushroom cultivation arena. By utilizing vertical space, growers can significantly increase their production capacity in a compact footprint. This method is particularly beneficial for urban settings where space is at a premium. Vertical farming systems, often combined with hydroponic or aeroponic techniques, allow for dense planting and can be integrated into existing infrastructure like warehouses or shipping containers. This innovation not only enhances productivity but also appeals to food and wellness entrepreneurs seeking to provide fresh, locally sourced mushrooms to their communities.

The rise of DIY mushroom growing kits has democratized mushroom cultivation, making it accessible to beginners and hobbyists. These kits often come with pre-inoculated substrates and easy-to-follow instructions, allowing individuals to cultivate gourmet and medicinal mushrooms at home.

Mushroom Millions: Fungi Fortunes from Small Spaces

This trend supports the side hustle entrepreneur, enabling them to tap into the burgeoning market for home-grown produce. Additionally, these kits foster a deeper connection to food and sustainability, encouraging consumers to engage with their food sources and explore the culinary and health benefits of mushrooms.

Finally, embracing online marketing strategies has become essential for mushroom entrepreneurs looking to reach a broader audience. Utilizing social media platforms, e-commerce websites, and educational content can effectively promote unique mushroom varieties and cultivation methods. By sharing knowledge and success stories, growers can build a community around their products, attracting customers who value transparency and sustainability. Innovations in marketing, combined with advancements in cultivation techniques, position mushroom growers to capitalize on the increasing demand for specialty mushrooms in restaurants, health markets, and home kitchens alike.

Mushroom Millions: Fungi Fortunes from Small Spaces

Market Predictions and Opportunities

The global mushroom market is experiencing significant growth, driven by an increasing demand for both culinary and medicinal varieties. Analysts predict that this sector will continue to expand in the coming years, fueled by a rising awareness of the health benefits associated with mushrooms, such as their nutritional value and potential therapeutic properties. As more consumers turn to plant-based diets and seek sustainable food sources, the opportunities for small-scale mushroom cultivation are vast and varied. Urban and suburban homesteaders can capitalize on this trend by establishing local production methods that cater to their communities while also reducing their carbon footprint.

Specialty mushroom varieties, such as oyster, lion's mane, and shiitake, are increasingly sought after by restaurants and chefs looking to enhance their menus with unique flavors and textures. As culinary trends shift towards gourmet ingredients, small-scale farmers can position themselves as local producers of these high-demand items.

Mushroom Millions: Fungi Fortunes from Small Spaces

By leveraging online marketing strategies, they can reach a wider audience and establish a brand that resonates with food and wellness enthusiasts. This niche not only offers potential for profit but also allows growers to participate in the growing movement towards sustainable food practices.

Home mushroom cultivation is becoming more accessible thanks to DIY mushroom growing kits that cater to beginners and those with limited space. These kits provide an excellent entry point for side hustle entrepreneurs looking to tap into the mushroom market without major upfront investments. With the right guidance and resources, aspiring growers can start producing gourmet mushrooms in their homes, potentially leading to a profitable venture. The simplicity of these kits makes them an attractive option for urban farmers who may not have traditional farming backgrounds but possess a passion for sustainable living.

Medicinal mushrooms represent another lucrative opportunity within the mushroom market. The increasing popularity of natural health products has led to a surge in demand for mushrooms like reishi, chaga, and cordyceps, known for their health benefits.

Mushroom Millions: Fungi Fortunes from Small Spaces

Entrepreneurs focusing on organic mushroom farming techniques can tap into this niche by producing high-quality products for health-conscious consumers. By educating themselves on the medicinal properties of these fungi, growers can effectively market their products to wellness enthusiasts and capitalize on the growing interest in holistic health solutions.

Finally, vertical farming solutions present an innovative approach to mushroom production that is particularly well-suited for urban environments. This method maximizes space and resources, making it possible to cultivate large quantities of mushrooms in a relatively small area. As technology continues to advance, integrating smart farming practices can further enhance productivity and sustainability. By adopting these modern techniques and embracing sustainable practices, growers can not only meet the rising demand for mushrooms but also contribute positively to their local ecosystems, ensuring a profitable future in this burgeoning market.

Mushroom Millions: Fungi Fortunes from Small Spaces

The Role of Technology in Mushroom Production

The integration of technology in mushroom production has transformed traditional farming practices, offering innovative solutions that cater to the needs of both small-scale farmers and urban growers. Advanced cultivation techniques have emerged, enabling enthusiasts to optimize their growing environments, monitor conditions, and enhance yields. Automation tools, such as climate control systems and humidity regulators, can significantly improve the efficiency of mushroom farming by maintaining ideal conditions for different species. This level of precision is especially beneficial for those operating in limited spaces, allowing for higher productivity without compromising quality.

The rise of data analytics in agriculture has also reached the realm of mushroom cultivation. Growers can now utilize sensors and software to track parameters such as temperature, humidity, and carbon dioxide levels in real-time. This data-driven approach allows for timely adjustments that can prevent crop loss and improve overall health. By analyzing growth patterns and environmental conditions, producers can refine their practices and select the most suitable mushroom varieties for their specific conditions.

Mushroom Millions: Fungi Fortunes from Small Spaces

This not only maximizes yield but also supports the sustainable practices that are increasingly important to consumers.

Vertical farming solutions have emerged as a game changer for mushroom production, particularly in urban settings where space is at a premium. These systems enable growers to stack production units, utilizing every available square foot while optimizing light and moisture distribution. Advanced hydroponic and aeroponic systems further enhance productivity, allowing mushrooms to thrive in controlled environments with minimal resource consumption. This innovative approach aligns with the growing interest in sustainable living, as it reduces land use and minimizes the carbon footprint associated with traditional farming methods.

Moreover, the development of DIY mushroom growing kits has made it easy for enthusiasts to enter the market with minimal investment. These kits often incorporate technology that simplifies the growing process, making it accessible for beginners. With pre-prepared substrates and inoculated spawn, users can cultivate gourmet and medicinal mushroom varieties right from their homes.

Mushroom Millions: Fungi Fortunes from Small Spaces

This democratization of mushroom farming not only empowers individuals to create their own food sources but also serves as an entry point for aspiring entrepreneurs looking to tap into the lucrative mushroom market.

Lastly, effective online marketing strategies have become essential for mushroom entrepreneurs seeking to reach broader audiences. With the rise of e-commerce, growers can leverage social media platforms and websites to showcase their products, share cultivation tips, and connect with potential customers. This direct-to-consumer approach fosters community engagement and allows small-scale farmers to build their brand around local, organic, and sustainable practices. The combination of technology in production and marketing offers a pathway for individuals to thrive in the mushroom industry, turning passion into profit while contributing to a more sustainable food system.

Chapter 13: Conclusion and Next Steps

Recap of Key Takeaways

The journey through the world of mushroom cultivation has unveiled valuable insights and strategies that empower growers and entrepreneurs alike. One of the primary takeaways is the immense potential of small-scale mushroom farming as a profitable venture. With the right techniques and understanding of market demands, individuals can cultivate gourmet and specialty mushroom varieties, catering to restaurants, local markets, and health-conscious consumers. This small-space farming opportunity allows for the production of high-value crops that can yield significant financial returns, even in urban settings.

Understanding the different types of mushrooms and their specific growing requirements is crucial for success. From oyster mushrooms to lion's mane and shiitake, each variety offers unique flavors, textures, and health benefits. The book emphasizes the importance of selecting the right species based on local demand and personal interests.

Mushroom Millions: Fungi Fortunes from Small Spaces

By focusing on specialty mushrooms that are not widely available in grocery stores, aspiring growers can carve out a niche in the marketplace, enhancing their profitability and establishing themselves as unique suppliers in their communities.

The implementation of sustainable practices is another key takeaway that aligns with the values of many modern consumers. Organic mushroom farming techniques, such as using natural substrates and minimizing chemical inputs, resonate well with the growing trend towards environmental consciousness. By adopting methods that promote sustainability, growers not only contribute to a healthier ecosystem but also appeal to a customer base that prioritizes organic and ethically produced food. This commitment to sustainability can serve as a powerful marketing tool, setting businesses apart in a competitive landscape.

For those venturing into mushroom cultivation as a side hustle or full-time endeavor, effective online marketing strategies are essential. The book provides insights into leveraging social media, creating engaging content, and building an online presence to reach potential customers.

Mushroom Millions: Fungi Fortunes from Small Spaces

By showcasing the uniqueness of their mushroom products and sharing their cultivation stories, entrepreneurs can foster a loyal customer base and drive sales. Understanding how to navigate e-commerce platforms and local food networks can further enhance visibility and accessibility to consumers.

Lastly, the importance of community and networking cannot be overstated. Engaging with local farmers' markets, joining mushroom cultivation clubs, and participating in workshops can provide invaluable support and knowledge exchange. Building connections with fellow growers and industry experts creates opportunities for collaboration, resource sharing, and mentorship. Embracing a community-oriented approach not only enriches the growing experience but also strengthens the overall mushroom farming ecosystem, fostering innovation and growth within the industry.

Mushroom Millions: Fungi Fortunes from Small Spaces

Resources for Continued Learning

In the evolving landscape of mushroom cultivation, continuous learning is essential for success. Various resources are available to enhance your knowledge and skills, catering specifically to global growers, small-scale farmers, and urban homesteaders. Books and online courses focused on mushroom cultivation provide foundational information, covering everything from basic growing techniques to advanced methods for cultivating specialty varieties. Notable authors and experts in the field have published comprehensive guides that delve into the intricacies of mushroom biology, cultivation techniques, and even the economic aspects of running a mushroom business.

Webinars and online workshops are increasingly popular among aspiring mushroom entrepreneurs. These interactive sessions often feature experienced growers and industry professionals who share insights on topics such as organic farming practices, sustainable growing methods, and marketing strategies tailored for the mushroom industry.

Mushroom Millions: Fungi Fortunes from Small Spaces

Platforms like YouTube also host a wealth of instructional videos, where viewers can watch step-by-step processes for setting up mushroom farms, creating DIY kits, and implementing vertical farming solutions. Engaging with these resources can help you keep up with the latest trends and innovations in mushroom farming.

Networking with fellow mushroom enthusiasts and professionals is another critical resource for continued learning. Joining local and online communities, such as forums and social media groups, allows you to share experiences, seek advice, and collaborate on projects. These networks often host events, such as mushroom forays and farmer's markets, providing opportunities for hands-on learning and direct interaction with seasoned growers. Participating in these communities can also open doors to mentorship opportunities, where you can gain personalized guidance from those with more experience in the field.

Mushroom Millions: Fungi Fortunes from Small Spaces

In addition to informal learning avenues, various organizations and associations dedicated to mushroom cultivation provide valuable resources. Many organizations offer certification programs that can enhance your credibility and marketability as a mushroom grower. These certifications often cover important topics like food safety standards and sustainable farming practices. Additionally, attending industry conferences can expose you to cutting-edge research and developments, as well as connect you to potential buyers, suppliers, and partners in the mushroom industry.

Finally, keeping abreast of scientific journals and publications related to fungi can significantly contribute to your understanding of mushroom cultivation. Research articles often present the latest findings on mushroom genetics, disease management, and the health benefits of different mushroom species. Staying informed through peer-reviewed journals helps you make evidence-based decisions in your farming practices, ensuring that your methods are both effective and sustainable. By leveraging these diverse resources, you can ensure that your mushroom venture remains innovative, profitable, and aligned with contemporary sustainable practices.

Mushroom Millions: Fungi Fortunes from Small Spaces

Encouragement for the Journey Ahead

As you embark on your journey into the world of mushroom cultivation, it's essential to recognize the unique opportunities that lie ahead. The mushroom industry is evolving rapidly, with an increasing demand for gourmet and specialty varieties that can thrive in urban settings. By tapping into this burgeoning market, you can create a sustainable business model that not only supports your financial goals but also contributes positively to your community's food systems. Embrace the potential of mushrooms as a lucrative venture that aligns with your passion for sustainable living and wellness.

The beauty of mushroom farming is its accessibility; even small spaces can yield impressive results. Whether you are a side hustle entrepreneur or a dedicated small-scale farmer, there are countless resources available to help you get started. DIY mushroom growing kits are an excellent option for beginners, allowing you to experiment with different species and growing techniques right in your kitchen or backyard.

www.farmers-library.com

Mushroom Millions: Fungi Fortunes from Small Spaces

As you gain experience, you will discover the nuances of organic mushroom farming, including the importance of environmental conditions, substrate selection, and maintenance routines that ensure healthy yields.

As you cultivate your mushrooms, consider the diverse markets that await your products. Gourmet mushrooms have become a staple in restaurants and among chefs who seek fresh, local ingredients. By establishing connections with local eateries and farmers' markets, you can create a steady customer base that appreciates the quality and flavor of your fungi. Additionally, the rising interest in medicinal mushrooms presents another avenue for exploration. Educating yourself about their benefits can position you as a knowledgeable supplier, tapping into the wellness trend that continues to gain momentum.

Sustainability is at the forefront of modern agricultural practices, and mushroom farming fits seamlessly into this narrative. By implementing sustainable techniques, such as vertical farming solutions, you can maximize your yield while minimizing your environmental footprint.

Mushroom Millions: Fungi Fortunes from Small Spaces

This not only enhances the marketability of your products but also resonates with consumers who prioritize eco-friendly practices. Sharing your sustainable journey through online platforms can attract like-minded individuals and create a community around your brand, fostering loyalty and support.

Lastly, as you navigate the challenges and successes of your mushroom venture, remember that entrepreneurship is a journey filled with learning and growth. Embrace the setbacks as opportunities to refine your techniques and marketing strategies. Engage with fellow growers, attend workshops, and utilize online resources to expand your knowledge. Each step you take brings you closer to realizing your vision of a flourishing mushroom business. With determination and creativity, you can transform your passion for fungi into a thriving enterprise that not only enriches your life but also contributes to a healthier and more sustainable world.

Printed in Dunstable, United Kingdom